M000087264

CONTENTS

ISBN 0-7935-1793-1

Hal Leonard Publishing Corporation
7777 West Bluemound Road P.O. Box 13819 Milwaukee, WI 53213

The Eight Days Of Chanukah

On the eve of the twenty fifth day of the Hebrew month of Kislev, Jews begin the eight days observance of Chanukah, the Festival of Lights, the Feast of Dedication. Chanukah is one of the most joyous festivals of the Jewish year – it commemorates the victory of the Maccabees in 165 B.C.E. over the Assyrians, then part of the Greek Empire. However, the holiday does not celebrate the military defeat of an enemy, but a moral victory in what was the first triumphant struggle ever waged for religious freedom. Chanukah also celebrates the rededication of the desecrated Temple in Jerusalem and the miracle of light.

Legend tells us that with only enough oil to rekindle the Temple lights for one day, the lights burned for eight days, thus the eight days of Chanukah.

Chanukah is the only Jewish holiday not mentioned in the Old Testament, but its traditions of latkes, dreidl, Chanukah gelt, and of course music, are universal among Jews.

Chanukah in our time is one of the happiest festivals on the Jewish calendar. It comes in the middle of winter, during the month of December, when the days are cold and harsh. Into this bleak month, Chanukah brings warmth and light and happiness. Homes are filled with a bright holiday spirit. The father lights the first candle with the "Shammes" (the serving candle) and he recites the blessings:

> "Blessed art Thou, O Lord, our God, Ruler of the Universe, who has sanctified us by Thy commandments and commanded us to kindle the light of Chanukah. Blessed art Thou, O Lord, our God, Ruler of the Universe, who performed miracles for our forefathers, in those days, at this season."

Chanukah is a holiday when families gather together to sing happy songs, such as we present in this book, for all ages to share and enjoy.

"Chanukah At Grover's Corner" Teaches Children
An Understanding Of Other Traditions

Public television has long been the leader in children's programs that stimulate, enlighten, and teach values. The latest example **is Chanukah at Grover's Corner,** a half-hour holiday special for children of all religious backgrounds airing winter of 1992.

Led by musician David Grover and Emmy Award-winning actor Theodore Bikel, **Chanukah at Grover's Corner** tells the story of the annual celebration of Chanukah through tales and original songs.

"Chanukah at Grover's Corner teaches kids about Chanukah, but it's more than just that," says producer Tim Paine. "The program is also about appreciating other traditions and encouraging people to learn about other cultures and religions." Bikel adds, "When people are curious about each other's culture and mores, they stop shouting at each other, and worse, shooting at each other."

The program takes place in Grover's Corner, a music store run by David Grover with help from his furry friend Mozart. Grover and Mozart—along with cast members Terry "A La Berry" Hall, Bev Rohlehr, and Kathy Jo Wartella—are visited by Bikel, Rabbi Alan Berg and a group of children. Together they celebrate the first day of Chanukah.

Preparation for the celebration is both musical and educational as the story of Chanukah slowly unfolds through stories and songs. The principal message is clear: it's fun—and important—to learn about other traditions, cultures, and celebrations.

Bikel, best known for his stage role as Tevye in *Fiddler on the Roof,* is a special guest at the Chanukah celebration. In addition to his stage performances, Bikel has appeared in some 35 films and several TV shows including a guest appearance on *Star Trek: The Next Generation.*

Performing has not been Bikel's sole interest. He has been active in human rights causes, funding for the arts, and is currently a Senior Vice President of the American Jewish Congress.

Grover has been performing for people of all ages for more than 20 years. A musician since early childhood, he has worked with Arlo Guthrie, Pete Seeger, Willie Nelson, John Denver, Hoyt Axton, and many others. Grover released his first collection of songs for and about children in 1988. "Light Up the World With Love," which he co-wrote with well-known songwriter Aaron Schroeder, includes the songs around which **Chanukah at Grover's Corner** was developed.

"There are many programs that teach children about Christmas," says Executive Producer Beth Curley. "We saw a real need on public television to present the story of Chanukah to children of all cultures. **Chanukah at Grover's Corner** fills that need."

David Grover

DAVID GROVER has been performing for more than twenty years, sharing songs and stories with people of all ages.

After years of playing solo and with various rock bands, Grover formed Shenandoah, a country-rock band which soon began touring with Arlo Guthrie. For six years he was guitarist, arranger and vocalist for Guthrie. During that time he played with Pete Seeger, Willie Nelson, John Denver, Hoyt Axton, and dozens of others, both as guitarist and opening act. He has toured extensively in the U.S. and abroad.

In 1981, Grover left the "road" to raise his daughter Jessica in the Berkshires of Western Massachusetts, write music full time, and teach. He met Aaron Schroeder who has a long successful career as a songwriter and record producer, and together they began a collaboration that has brought local acclaim with community ˜ntributions, national and international acclaim ˜ongs in pop and gospel markets, children's ˜V series, and films. In 1984, he released

his first album of original music (written with Schroeder) on the Big Bear label, "If I Could Only Touch Your Life," the title song of which was also recorded by Arlo Guthrie and released on Warner Brothers Records that same year.

Through his daughter, Grover began to get more and more involved in children's music, both as a performer and as a writer. He quickly found a niche in children's music and toured, first throughout New England and the U.S., and later on to the People's Republic of China, sharing music with the children there and proving that music is indeed a universal language.

In 1988, he released another album penned with Schroeder, "Kids Mean The World To Us," which became popular with parents and children. Since then three other albums of children's music have been released, with many original songs by Grover and Schroeder: "One World" – songs from America and other places; "I'll Be Your Friend" – more songs for friendly kids; and "Light Up The World With Love" – songs for Christmas and Chanukah.

It was the latter that became the springboard for the television show **Chanukah at Grover's Corner.**

In addition to the television show **Grover's Corner,** Grover's video **One World** was released as the National Song of PBS's "Operation Earth" in 1989.

Grover has been writing songs with Aaron Schroeder for grown-ups and kids for years. Some of their credits include recordings by Barry White, Arlo Guthrie, Tramaine Hawkins (their song "We're All In The Same Boat" was nominated for a 1989 Dove Award for Traditional Gospel Song of the Year) and in 1991, they wrote and produced the music for the movie, and in 1992 the TV series, "Lucky Luke" starring Terence Hill. In 1991, Grover also produced "Son of the Wind," Arlo Guthrie's new album.

Aaron Schroeder

AARON SCHROEDER writes songs that span generations. His career is truly a reflection of the modern music world. Beginning with Aaron's sixteen song contributions to the Presley legend (including five #1 hits: "It's Now Or Never," "Stuck On You," "Good Luck Charm," "I Got Stung," and "A Big Hunk O' Love"), on to the 1992 smash "Move Me No Mountain" by Soul II Soul, Aaron's hits cover four decades of ever changing musical tastes.

From rhythm and blues to country music, Frank Sinatra to Chaka Khan, Roy Orbison to Dionne Warwick, Aaron's songs have appeared on national and international charts garnering gold and platinum records and illustrating a rare versatility and longevity.

Most recently, Aaron has been working with songwriter/performer, David Grover. Their material ranges from children's cassettes and videos (like the 1992 PBS special "Chanukah at Grover's Corner") to writing and producing the soundtrack and original songs for "Lucky Luke,"

the movie and television series, presently on a successful release schedule around the world.

Schroeder and Grover have written for Barry White, Tramaine Hawkins, and Arlo Guthrie, as well as David's many recordings. They have been nominated for and have received major awards in both the record and television fields.

As an international music publisher, Aaron is known for his innovations and creativity. He holds an unsurpassed record for discovering, guiding and developing such great composers and lyricists as Randy Newman, Barry White, Irwin Levine, Jimi Hendrix, Fred Neil, and Gene Pitney.

A highly regarded record producer, Mr. Schroeder founded Musicor Records, a forerunner of the independent labels to be distributed by major companies worldwide. He produced the Academy Award nominee, "Town Without Pity," and the first album by the legendary Blood, Sweat and Tears. He conceived the marriage of the Pitney sound with the songwriting team of Burt Bacharach and Hal David resulting in a string of Gene Pitney hits like "The Man Who Shot Liberty Valance," "Only Love Can Break A Heart," and "Twenty-Four Hours From Tulsa."

Having made his mark in every other popular category, Aaron is presently at work planning his next major project…a stage musical.

Aaron Schroeder is listed in Who's Who.

HAYOM CHANUKAH

Words and Music by AARON SCHROEDER
and DAVID GROVER

*Pickup notes to be sung/played before Part 3 only.

The Miracle Of The Menorah

Over two thousand years ago, the land where the Jewish people lived was invaded. They were told they couldn't practice their own religion anymore. It seemed hopeless, the other countries had big armies and the Jews were no match for them; but they would not give up their beliefs and they fought hard for their freedom. They were led by a man named Judah Maccabee. He inspired his people to fight for their human rights. Lo and behold, they defeated the other big armies and won the right to practice their own religion. Chanukah is the festival when we remember that fight and those brave people and we celebrate their victory. And Chanukah is even more than that…

David Grover and some of his friends at "Grover's Corner" listen as Theodore Bikel explains the historical story of the Chanukah miracle of light.

Rabbi Alan Berg (center) gathers with the cast of the PBS television special, Chanukah At Grover's Corner, to explain the significance of lighting the Menorah, a candle a day for the eight-day holiday.

THE MIRACLE OF THE MENORAH

Words and Music by AARON SCHROEDER
and DAVID GROVER

2.(Spoken:) When Judah Maccabee freed the city of Jerusalem, oil was needed to light the Menorah in the temple. Just a little bit was found,

1.(Spoken:) Chanukah is a celebration of light.
only enough for one night, but by a miracle it burned for

Latkes

Some people believe that the Maccabees ate Latkes because potatoes were available to their army and they could be prepared so quickly. Other people think that the oil the latkes are cooked in symbolizes the oil which burned for eight days.

Theodore Bikel teaches Mozart, David Grover's puppet pal, how to prepare potato latkes on the PBS television special, Chanukah At Grover's Corner.

LATKES

Words and Music by AARON SCHROEDER
and DAVID GROVER

cal and low cho - les - ter - ol Cha - nu - kah,

rit.

a tempo

Moderately bright

food.

Lat - kes, lat - kes,

I love lat - kes; not a lit - tle, but a lot of lat - kes.

Lat - kes, lat - kes, I love lat - kes; not a lit - tle, but a

The Dreidl Song

When Antiochus the Syrian king forbade the Jews to study the Torah, they met secretly in small groups and studied anyway and learned the Torah by heart. One of the ways they avoided being caught was to keep a little top on the table while they were studying. If a soldier appeared, one of the group would spin the dreidl and all of them would pretend they were playing an exciting game. Since the soldiers could not prove otherwise, the little Chanukah dreidl saved many lives and preserved the religious study of the Jewish people.

THE DREIDL SONG

Words and Music by AARON SCHROEDER
and DAVID GROVER

What do you say let's play Drei - dl.

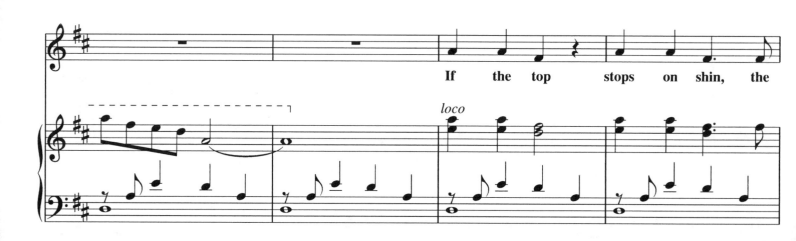

If the top stops on shin, the

play - er puts an - oth - er pen - ny in. What do you say

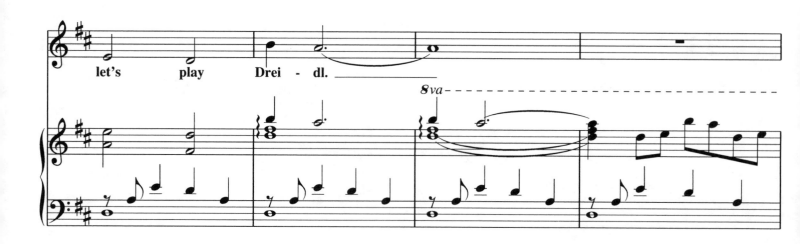

let's play Drei - dl.

SPIN! SPIN! SPIN!

Words and Music by AARON SCHROEDER
and DAVID GROVER

CHANUKAH GELT

Words and Music by AARON SCHROEDER
and DAVID GROVER

34

CHANUKAH SIM SHALOM

Words and Music by AARON SCHROEDER
and DAVID GROVER

CHANUKAH

Words and Music by AARON SCHROEDER
and DAVID GROVER

Happily, in-two

Lyrics:

(1.,4.) Cha - nu - kah, Cha - nu - kah, oh what joy you bring. Cha - nu - kah, Cha - nu - kah, time to dance and sing.

(2.) La la la, la la la, la la la la la. La la la, la la la, la la la la la.

(3.) Cha - nu - kah, Cha - nu - kah, makes me feel so good. Cha - nu - kah, Cha - nu - kah, don't you think it should.

ZUM GALLI GALLI

Words and Music by AARON SCHROEDER
and DAVID GROVER

Pickup notes to be sung/played before Part 2 only.

Blood Of The Maccabees

On the morning after Judah Maccabee was slain in battle, lovely white flowers flecked with blood-red dots sprouted on the battlefield. People called these blossoms "Blood of the Maccabees." To this very day they grow in the hills of Judea covering the mountain sides with beautiful clusters of red and white, which are startling to behold.

Each year at Chanukah, children in Israel climb the hills to pick flowers for their holiday celebrations. Among the flowers they seek are the Blood of the Maccabees, the red and white symbols of the courage of Judah Maccabee.

BLOOD OF THE MACCABEES

Words and Music by AARON SCHROEDER
and DAVID GROVER

THE EIGHT DAYS OF CHANUKAH

Words and Music by AARON SCHROEDER
and DAVID GROVER

52

LIGHT UP THE WORLD WITH LOVE

Words and Music by AARON SCHROEDER
and DAVID GROVER

60

A Glossary Of Terms From Chanukah At Grover's Corner

CHANUKAH
"The Festival Of Lights" - Literally means "Dedication." A holiday which begins on the evening of the 25th day of the Hebrew month of Kislev and commemorates the liberation and the rededication of the ancient temple in Jerusalem by Judah Maccabee and his followers.

DREIDL (Dreydel)
A four sided top used in a game played during Chanukah. Each side is marked with a different Hebrew letter. It is a game of put and take using pennies or nuts. Every participant puts one penny or nut into the "pot." The children then take turns spinning the dreidl.

The letters on the Dreidl:

> *Nun* - the 14th letter of the Hebrew alphabet which stands for "nicht," or "none." If the dreidl stops on Nun, the player takes nothing from the pot.
>
> *Shin* - the 22nd letter of the Hebrew alphabet which stands for "shtell," or "put." If the dreidl stops on Shin, the player puts money into the pot.
>
> *Hay* - the 5th letter of the Hebrew alphabet which stands for "halb," or "half." If the dreidl stops on Hay, the player wins half of the pot.
>
> *Gimel* - the 3rd letter of the Hebrew alphabet which stands for "gantz," or "all." The lucky dreidl player whose dreidl stops on Gimel wins the entire pot.

The letters also stand for the phrase "Nes gadol hayah shan" or "A great miracle happened there."

ESS - To eat

FRESS - To eat and eat (overeat - stuff yourself)

GEFILTE FISH - A Jewish dish of stewed or baked fish stuffed with a mixture of the fish flesh, bread crumbs, eggs, and seasonings prepared as balls or oval cakes boiled in a fish stock.

GELT - Money, sometimes given instead of presents on Chanukah. In the dreidl game, the pot is referred to as "gelt."

* Kopek - A small copper Russian coin; there are one hundred Kopeks in a Ruble
* Grivnye - A silver Russian coin worth ten Kopeks
* Ruble - Formerly a Russian silver coin, later a piece of paper money
* Groschen - A small German silver coin about two cents
* Gulden - An Austrian silver coin worth about forty eight cents

* coins used early in the twentieth century

JUDAH MACCABEE - Leader of the Maccabean revolt, one of five sons of Mattathias. He led the Judeans to victory and rededicated the temple which the Syrians had desecrated.

LATKES - Delicious potato pancakes made from grated raw potato, traditionally served during the Chanukah celebration.

MENORAH - A candelabrum with nine candle holders. Eight candles are lit, one on each night of Chanukah. The ninth candle holds the "Shamus", which is used to light the others.

RABBI - The spiritual leader of a Jewish congregation who performs various duties such as teaching, officiating at ceremonies, and leading services.

TORAH - Book of Jewish teaching of laws, customs and ceremonies.

SHALOM - A Jewish greeting or farewell. It also means well-being and peace.

Discography Of David Grover Recordings

IF I COULD ONLY TOUCH YOUR LIFE [Big Bear - BB 0100]
Take Your Time; Let Me Put The Love Back In Your Life;
Doesn't Take Much To Make You Happy; The Teddy Bears' Picnic;
The Saga Of Luther The Dog; It's Always Like The First Time;
Tennessee Sunshine; One Life One Love; Summer Sweetheart;
If I Could Only Touch Your Life; Get Together

KIDS MEAN THE WORLD TO US [Big Bear - BB 0200]
Ezra The Stripeless Zebra; It's A Small World; Bingo;
The Garden Song; Riding In My Car; I Love My Rooster;
Hushabye; Be Yourself; Abiyo-yo; My Mommy Comes Back;
What Do I Do?; Kid's Mean The World To Us

ONE WORLD [Big Bear - BB 0300]
The Hello Song; Zip-A-Dee Doo Dah; Jambo; The Buenas Song;
Polly Put The Kettle On; Sim Shalom; Hot Dang Dilly;
May There Always Be Sunshine; I Won't Grow Up;
I Love The Earth; The Sun And The Moon; One World

LIGHT UP THE WORLD WITH LOVE [Big Bear - BB 0400]
Ernestine The Green-Eyed Elf; We Wish You A Merry Christmas;
Santa Claus Is Coming To Town; Rudolf The Red Nosed Reindeer;
Hey Ho Nobody Home; The Little Drummer Boy; Christmas All Over
The World; Santa Musta Got Up On The Wrong Side Of The Sleigh
Today; Hayom Chanukah; The Miracle Of The Menorah; Latkes;
The Dreidl Song; The Eight Days Of Chanukah; Light Up The
World With Love; We're All Americans

I'LL BE YOUR FRIEND [Big Bear - BB 0500]
I'll Be Your Friend; I Wake Up In The Morning; Aquarium;
50's Fun; Hole In The Bottom Of The Sea; Weaver Of Dreams;
I Wish That I Could Be The Sun; This Little Light Of Mine;
Vadee Veedee Videe Vodee Voo; Hole In The Bucket; Twinkle
Twinkle Little Star Medley; God Loves You And Me; There's A
Little Band A' Playin' In My Heart; All Through The Night

All Recordings Are Available Through Big Bear Records,
P.O. Box 532, North Egremont, MA. 01252